BASKETBALL'S GREATEST STARS

JAMES HARDEN

Teasdell

SportsZone

An Imprint of Abdo Publishing
abdopublishing.com

abdopublishing.com

Published by Abdo Publishing, a division of ABDO, PO Box 398166, Minneapolis, Minnesota 55439. Copyright © 2017 by Abdo Consulting Group, Inc. International copyrights reserved in all countries. No part of this book may be reproduced in any form without written permission from the publisher. SportsZone™ is a trademark and logo of Abdo Publishing.

Printed in the United States of America, North Mankato, Minnesota
082016
012017

Cover Photos: Bob Levey/AP Images, background; David J. Phillip/AP Images, foreground
Interior Photos: Bob Levey/AP Images, 1 (background); David J. Phillip/AP Images, 1 (foreground), 25; Manu Fernandez/AP Images, 4-5; Alvaro Barrientos/AP Images, 6; Emilio Morenatti/AP Images, 7; Tom Luksys/Sportida/SIPA/AP Images, 8-9; Rich Pedroncelli/AP Images, 10-11; Nick Doan/Icon SMI/Newscom, 12; AJ Mast/Icon Sportswire, 13; Matt A. Brown/Icon Sportswire, 14-15; Nick Doan/Icon Sportswire, 16-17; Jason DeCrow/AP Images, 18-19; Bahram Mark Sobhani/AP Images, 20-21; Sue Ogrocki/AP Images, 22-23; Jeffrey Phelps/AP Images, 24; Marc Serota/AP Images, 26-27; Juanjo Martin/EPA/Newscom, 28-29

Editor: Todd Kortemeier
Series Designer: Laura Polzin

Publisher's Cataloging-in-Publication Data
Names: Trusdell, Brian, author.
Title: James Harden / by Brian Trusdell.
Description: Minneapolis, MN : Abdo Publishing, 2017. | Series: Basketball's greatest stars | Includes index.
Identifiers: LCCN 2016945489 | ISBN 9781680785456 (lib. bdg.) | ISBN 9781680798081 (ebook)
Subjects: LCSH: Harden, James, 1989- --Juvenile literature. | Basketball players--United States--Biography--Juvenile literature.
Classification: DDC 796.323 [B]--dc23
LC record available at http://lccn.loc.gov/2016945489

CONTENTS

FEAR THE BEARD 4

ROUGH START 10

RISING SUN DEVIL 14

OFF TO OKLAHOMA 18

A MOVE TO HOUSTON 22

GLOBAL IMPACT 26

Timeline 30
Glossary 31
Index 32
About the Author 32

FEAR THE BEARD

James Harden passed the ball to his Team USA teammate, Anthony Davis. Harden got the ball right back, drove to the basket, and hit a layup.

Ninety seconds later, Harden drained a three-pointer. Thirty seconds after that, Harden had a fast-break layup. Suddenly Harden seemed to be everywhere, and his opponents had no way to stop him.

James Harden looks on as Team USA battles Lithuania at the 2014 Basketball World Cup.

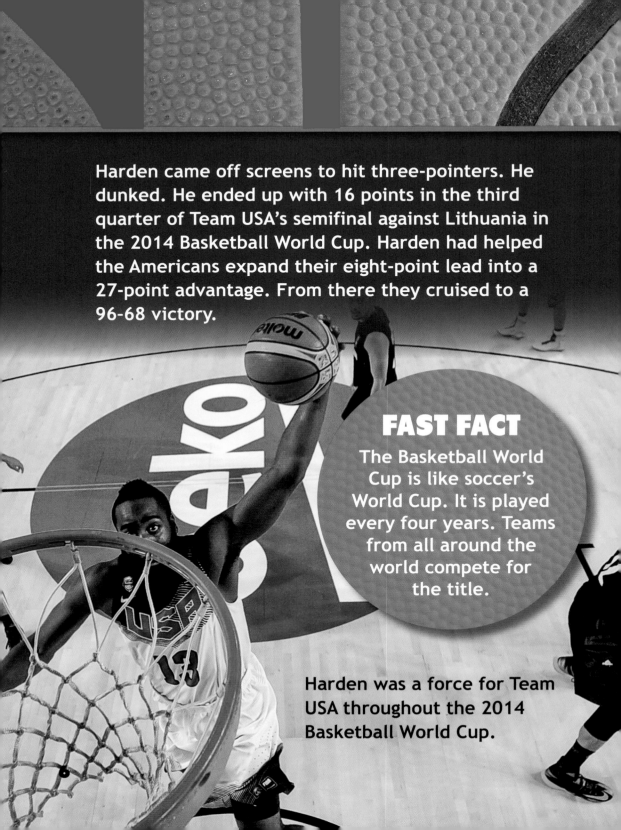

Harden came off screens to hit three-pointers. He dunked. He ended up with 16 points in the third quarter of Team USA's semifinal against Lithuania in the 2014 Basketball World Cup. Harden had helped the Americans expand their eight-point lead into a 27-point advantage. From there they cruised to a 96-68 victory.

FAST FACT

The Basketball World Cup is like soccer's World Cup. It is played every four years. Teams from all around the world compete for the title.

Harden was a force for Team USA throughout the 2014 Basketball World Cup.

Harden goes for a block against Lithuania.

The 6-foot-5 guard with a left-handed jump shot and trademark bushy beard carried Team USA into the championship game. But he was about to become a world champion.

The world basketball community found out why NBA teams had little choice but to "Fear the Beard."

FAST FACT

Harden's beard started as a goatee in college. He said it started because he felt too lazy to shave regularly.

Harden raises the Naismith Trophy after the United States defeated Serbia in the 2014 Basketball World Cup Final.

ROUGH START

Harden grew up near Los Angeles in crime-ridden Compton, California. His dad, James Harden Sr., was in the Navy but then was in and out of jail.

His mother, Monja Willis, wanted her son to go to a better school, so she enrolled James at Artesia High School in nearby Lakewood. He made the varsity basketball team in his freshman year.

James Harden, *right*, celebrates with teammate Malik Story after leading Artesia High School to a state championship victory in 2006.

FAST FACT

Harden has two older siblings. His half-brother, Akili Roberson, played quarterback for the University of Kansas.

In his junior and senior years, James led Artesia to consecutive state championships. He received scholarship offers from several colleges. He chose Arizona State because his former coach, Scott Pera, had left Artesia after Harden's junior year to become an assistant coach there.

Harden decided that Arizona State would be the best fit for him.

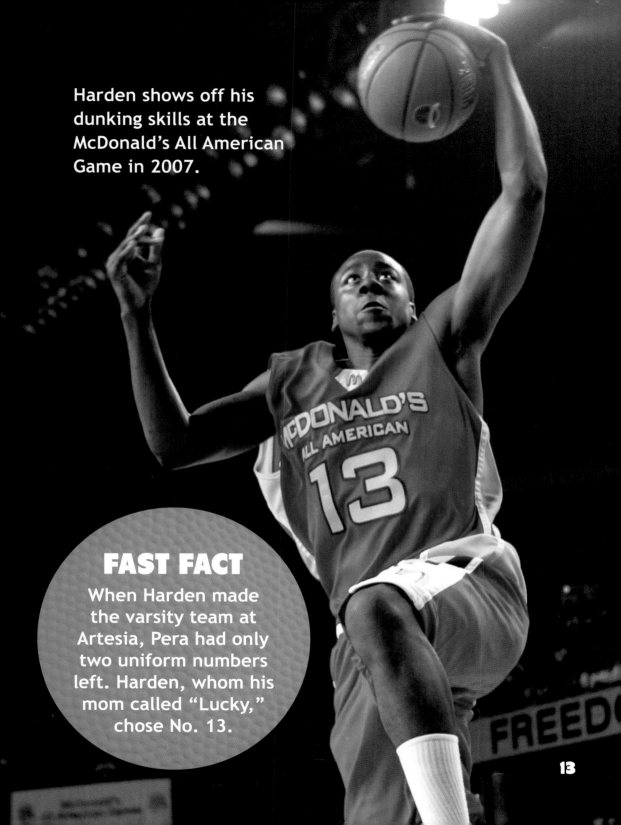

Harden shows off his dunking skills at the McDonald's All American Game in 2007.

FAST FACT

When Harden made the varsity team at Artesia, Pera had only two uniform numbers left. Harden, whom his mom called "Lucky," chose No. 13.

RISING SUN DEVIL

Arizona State was coming off back-to-back losing seasons when Harden arrived on campus in 2007. In his first season, he averaged 17.8 points per game and helped the Sun Devils to a 21-13 record. He earned first-team honors in the Pac-10 Conference.

FAST FACT

In 2015 Arizona State retired Harden's No. 13. He was the seventh player so honored by the university.

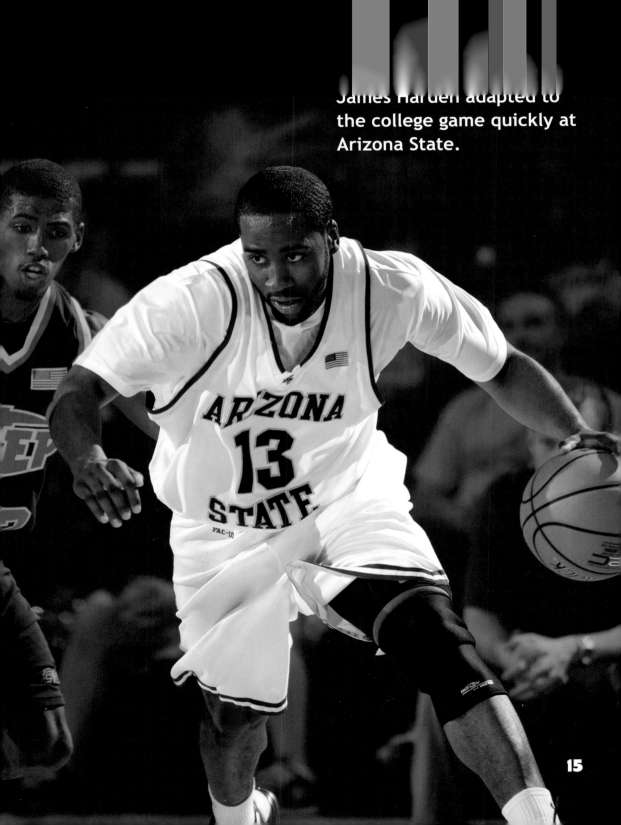

James Harden adapted to the college game quickly at Arizona State.

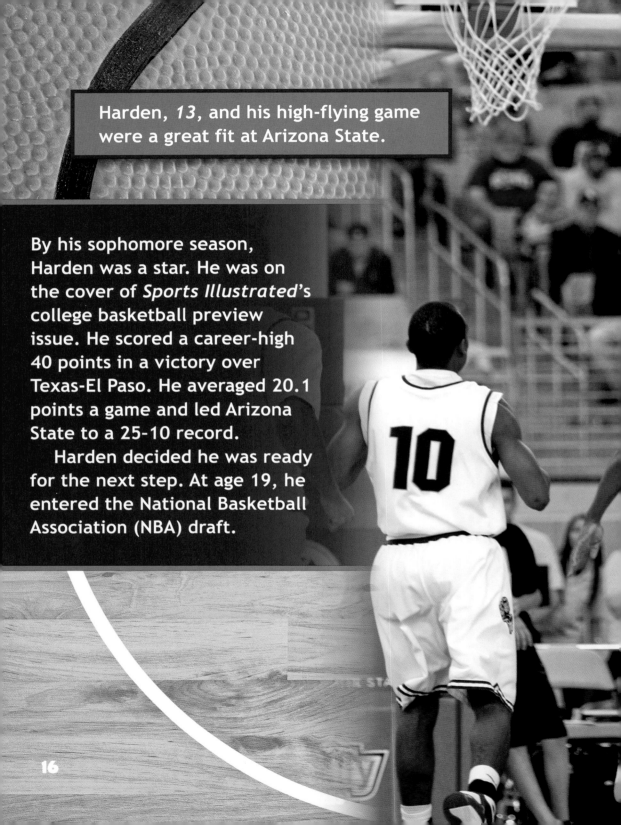

Harden, *13*, and his high-flying game were a great fit at Arizona State.

By his sophomore season, Harden was a star. He was on the cover of *Sports Illustrated*'s college basketball preview issue. He scored a career-high 40 points in a victory over Texas-El Paso. He averaged 20.1 points a game and led Arizona State to a 25-10 record.

Harden decided he was ready for the next step. At age 19, he entered the National Basketball Association (NBA) draft.

FAST FACT

Harden was the Pac-10's Player of the Year in his sophomore year. He helped the Sun Devils reach the NCAA tournament for the first time in six years.

OFF TO OKLAHOMA

Harden wore a three-piece suit and bow tie. His beard was trimmed. He answered reporters' questions with a broad smile.

He had just been selected by the Oklahoma City Thunder with the third pick in the 2009 NBA Draft.

FAST FACT

The Seattle SuperSonics moved to Oklahoma City in 2008 and the owners changed the team's name to the Thunder.

James Harden was all smiles after being drafted by the Oklahoma City Thunder on June 25, 2009.

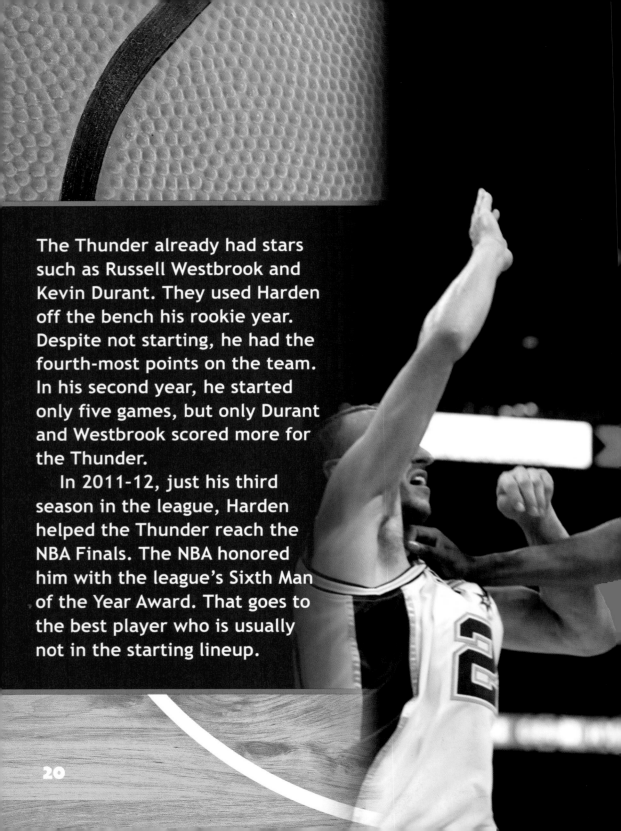

The Thunder already had stars such as Russell Westbrook and Kevin Durant. They used Harden off the bench his rookie year. Despite not starting, he had the fourth-most points on the team. In his second year, he started only five games, but only Durant and Westbrook scored more for the Thunder.

In 2011-12, just his third season in the league, Harden helped the Thunder reach the NBA Finals. The NBA honored him with the league's Sixth Man of the Year Award. That goes to the best player who is usually not in the starting lineup.

Harden continued to be an effective scorer when he reached the NBA.

FAST FACT

Although five play at one time, a basketball team is made up of more players. The "sixth man" is the best of a team's reserve players.

A MOVE TO HOUSTON

The 2012-13 season was approaching. Harden had a year remaining on his contract with Oklahoma City. The Thunder knew Harden deserved a lot more money. But they also had to pay Durant and Westbrook. They could not afford to pay all three what they were worth. So the Thunder traded Harden to the Houston Rockets.

FAST FACT

The San Diego Rockets began play in 1967. They moved to Houston in 1971. The team's nickname worked in its new home— Houston is the location of the NASA Space Center.

James Harden became the focal point of the Rockets' offense when he was traded to Houston.

In Houston Harden immediately became a starter. He scored 37 points in his first game. Two days later he poured in 45. He was picked for his first NBA All-Star Game.

Harden led the Rockets in scoring in each of his first four seasons in Houston. He also made the All-Star Game every year. He finished second in the voting for the league's Most Valuable Player (MVP) Award in the 2014-15 season.

Harden, *right*, battles Milwaukee's Luc Richard Mbah a Moute for a loose ball in a 2013 game.

A young fan supports Harden's MVP campaign late in the 2014-15 season.

FAST FACT

By 2012 Harden's beard had grown long and thick. Fans began attending games wearing fake beards and "Fear the Beard" T-shirts.

GLOBAL IMPACT

Harden was selected to represent the United States at the 2012 Olympic Games in London. The roster also included several players from the team that had won gold four years earlier. Kobe Bryant and LeBron James were the stars of the team. Harden, just 22 years old, was the second-youngest player on the team.

He played in all eight of Team USA's games, but he totaled only 74 minutes on the floor. Still, he scored 44 points and helped the United States win another gold medal.

James Harden played a supporting role for Team USA at the 2012 Olympic Games.

Harden, *right*, celebrates with Kyrie Irving after Team USA's blowout victory over Serbia in the 2014 Basketball World Cup title game.

Two years later, Bryant and James decided not to play at the Basketball World Cup. Coach Mike Krzyzewski needed a new leader for the team. Harden was the right man for the job. He scored a team-high 14.2 points per game as Team USA went 9-0 in the tournament. After his outburst in the semifinal against Lithuania, Harden scored 23 points against Serbia in the final. Team USA won 129-92.

Whether in Houston or on the international stage, Harden has shown that he's more than just a player with a beard. He's one of the best scorers in the world.

FAST FACT

The United States
has not always treated
the World Cup as a major
tournament. Still, it has
won the tournament
five times, tied with
Yugoslavia/Serbia for
the most titles.

TIMELINE

1989
James Edward Harden Jr. is born on August 26 in Bellflower, California.

2003
Harden makes the varsity basketball team as a freshman at Artesia High School.

2009
At Arizona State, Harden is named Pacific-10 Conference Player of the Year. On June 25, he is drafted third overall by the Oklahoma City Thunder.

2012
The Thunder trade Harden to the Houston Rockets on October 27.

2012
Harden and Team USA win gold in men's basketball at the London Olympics on August 12.

2013
Harden scores 15 points on 6-for-13 shooting in his first All-Star Game in front of his home fans in Houston on February 17.

2014
Harden leads Team USA in scoring as the United States wins the Basketball World Cup in Spain.

2015
On April 1, Harden scores a career-high 51 points to lead Houston over the Sacramento Kings.

GLOSSARY

CAMPUS
The grounds of a school.

CONTRACT
An agreement to play for a certain team.

DRAFT
The process by which leagues determine which teams can sign new players coming into the league.

GOATEE
A small beard.

LAYUP
A shot made from close to the basket; an easy shot.

ROSTER
A list of players that make up a team.

SCHOLARSHIP
Money given to a student to pay for education expenses.

SCREEN
When an offensive player legally blocks the path of a defender to open up a teammate for a shot or a pass; also called a pick.

TRADEMARK
A unique or distinctive feature or characteristic.

INDEX

Arizona State University, 12, 14, 15, 16, 17

Bryant, Kobe, 26, 28

Compton, California, 10

Davis, Anthony, 4
Durant, Kevin, 20, 22

Harden, James, Sr., 10
Houston Rockets, 22, 23, 24
Houston, Texas, 22, 24, 28

Irving, Kyrie, 28

James, LeBron, 26, 28

Krzyzewski, Mike, 28

Lakewood, California, 10
Los Angeles, California, 10

Mbah a Moute, Luc Richard, 24
Milwaukee Bucks, 24

Oklahoma City Thunder, 18, 20, 22

Pera, Scott, 12, 13

Roberson, Akili, 11

San Diego Rockets, 22
Seattle SuperSonics, 18
Story, Malik, 10

Westbrook, Russell, 20, 22
Willis, Monja, 10

ABOUT THE AUTHOR

Brian Trusdell has been a sports writer for more than 30 years with the Associated Press and Bloomberg News. He lives in New Jersey with his wife.